Goodbye, Regret

Forgiving Yourself of Past Mistakes

Doris Swift

Goodbye, Regret
Forgiving Yourself of Past Mistakes
By Doris Swift

Copyright © 2016 by Doris Swift
dorisswift.com
Cover photo: iStock photo ID:46886018
Author picture by: Karen Anne Crusco
Edited by: Tara Cole

ISBN:
978-1530996773
1530996775

To all the women who feel their past mistakes define them.
I pray this message offers renewed hope and freedom beyond your wildest dreams.

To my Lord and Savior, Jesus Christ. I'd be lost without You.

"When one door of happiness closes, another opens; but often we look so long at the closed door that we do not see the one which has opened for us."
~ Helen Keller

Contents

PART I

We've All Experienced Regret

We've all

made mistakes,

experienced regret,

wish we had…

...and wish we hadn't.

But wishing won't change the past, will it?

And we remember standing at the crossroad before making that choice. As the past seeps into the present, we wonder if consequences will fall like dominoes into the future.

Then we worry.

And we question.

And we doubt.

We doubt our decisions, don't we?

We question if we're in God's will or if we've plowed right through His road blocks. Did we miss a detour?

Have you been there?

I've been there on that road of doubt, and it stings like a bee because our decisions affect our loved ones too.

And we wonder, how long?

How long will the ripples travel outward from the first drop of our mistakes? Were they even mistakes at all?

And then we dwell.

We dwell on the past which we cannot change. Our thoughts circle round the what ifs and if onlys, and our souls become parched in the…

Sea of Regret.

And isn't it ironic?

Because a sea shouldn't be so dry.

PART II

The Woman, the Well,
and the How

So how do we let go?

What does that even mean?

Jesus met that woman at the well.

What if that woman did everything right?

Would she have been at that well,
at that time of day, at that very place?

Would she have met Jesus if she didn't need grace?

That woman...

Five husbands in her past and now another who was not her husband.

She was scandalous. An outcast.

She ventured out for water in the midday heat, avoiding those early-morning women and those early-evening women, perhaps because they whispered and mocked.

Does it make us cringe?

Do we cringe because we feel her shame and feel her pain? Or do we cringe…

…because we're the whispering mockers.

And shouldn't we be cringing for ourselves?

Why?

*Because before we can be made clean,
we've got to come clean.*

And that woman?

We may say it was shame that timed her journey
to the well that day.

Truth is…

…divine encounters meet us in our shame, in our regret, in our past mistakes, in our poor decisions,

in our sin.

So how does this letting go of past mistakes and letting go of Goliath-sized regret work?

The answer is Jesus.
He is our hope, and He is our strength.

HE IS.

But who *is* He?

How do we know Him?

We take a journey into God's Living Word.

The Bible. When we do, we learn this:

He put on flesh and dwelt among us.

He knit us together in our mother's womb.

We are made in His image, and He is beautiful.

He is Jesus. He is the **Son of God**.

He is **God the Son**.

He is **God**.

HE IS.

And He loves us unconditionally…

…right where we are.

Jesus is the way, the truth, and the life. He is Lord, Savior, Redeemer, Deliverer, Friend. His love will change your life because this doesn't sound like living:

I feel so…

ugly   alone   guilty

lost   afraid

weary   unworthy   worthless

worried   helpless

insecure   *hopeless*   ashamed

unlovable   invisible

insignificant

confused   abandoned

unwanted

regretful   unloved

And we can all relate to this…

I can't forgive.

I dwell on past mistakes.

I will never be good enough.

I am overwhelmed by regret.

I can't be forgiven of *that* sin.

I am a failure. I am bitter. I am broken.

Are you ready to be free?

In God's Word we find beautiful encounters with Jesus recorded to show us He knows us better than we know ourselves, and He wants us to know Him.

Personally.

He is the only way to the Father, and He shows us how to pray.

And we pray to understand what God wants to teach us, and how He wants to reach us.

So how about…

…we stop all the dwelling on what could have been, and if only we had, and if only we hadn't.

Because what if…

…we've grown far stronger,

loved far deeper,

and learned far greater,

from what we've done wrong
than from what we've done right?

Jesus said to that woman at the well:

"…*If you knew the gift of God, and who it is who says to you, 'Give Me a drink,' you would have asked Him, and He would have given you living water.*"   *John 4:10*

Living Water...

…will quench our parched souls
and pull us free from the sea of regret.

And this woman was amazed.
How did He know all she had ever done?

And this Jesus? He knew more than just her past mistakes…

He knew who He created her to be.

She left her (*shame, past mistakes, regret,…*) water pot behind,
went straight into the city and said to the men,

"Could this be the Messiah?"

She believed, and she was changed.
When we believe, we are changed.

She encountered *real love.* She was set free.

She had a new identity.

"Blessed is she who has believed that the Lord would fulfill His promises to her!"
Luke 1:45 (NIV)

And this Samaritan woman?

We can learn a lesson from her...

She could not contain her encounter with Jesus.
She went straight into the city and made Him known.

Many believed in Him that day because of
the word of her *testimony…*

"And many of the Samaritans of that city believed in Him because of the word of the woman who testified,'He told me all that I ever did.' So when the Samaritans had come to Him, they urged Him to stay with them; and He stayed there two days. And many more believed because of His own word."
John 4:39-41

Her past did not hinder her purpose.

She had been with Jesus, and it showed on her face. Her life of disgrace was transformed…

by *GRACE.*

And people noticed.

Some have been to the well,

and some have yet to journey there.

But we all sin and we all fall short,

and isn't that what grace is for?

And when we've been to that well we have a
story to tell, but first we must do this:

Forgive others and forgive ourselves.

Because no matter our story.

No matter our past mistakes.

No matter our regret and human missteps.

Our past story does not discredit our Grace Story...

...it becomes part of it.

So forgive,

and believe,

and trust…

…because God works all of it

together for our good.

All of it.

PART III

Turn of Events

Did you know?
There's an enemy who wants us to stay defeated.

But he has no power unless we give it to him by drifting away from the One who has all the power.

Have we forgotten who our Father is?

So the next time the enemy of our soul
whispers those reminders of regret,

and the next time we catch ourselves saying,
"*If only I had…*"

and the next time we dwell on past mistakes,
and beat ourselves up,
and put ourselves down…

let's remember, we can't undo what has been done.
We can't fight the enemy on our own.

But God…

…can take what's been done and shower grace upon it.

"I, even I, am He who blots out your
transgressions for My own sake;
And I will not remember your sins…"
Isaiah 43:25

We don't have to forget where we've been,
but we need to remember
we don't live there anymore.

And that enemy who wants to
shut us down and chew us up?

When we are in Christ, the enemy cannot defeat us.

*"Therefore submit to **God**.*
Resist the devil and he will flee from you."
James 4:7

And here's more bold truth:

"...because He who is in you is greater
than he who is in the world." *1 John 4:4*

Aren't you glad?

When we dwell on past mistakes,
we have not forgiven ourselves.

Because dwelling on past mistakes is a mistake.

"...there is now no condemnation for those who are in Christ Jesus, because through Christ Jesus the law of the Spirit who gives life has set you free from the law of sin and death." Romans 8:1-2 (NIV)

When we idle in the past,
the past becomes our idol.

"Forget the former things;
do not dwell on the past.
See, I am doing a new thing!
Now it springs up;
do you not perceive it?
I am making a way in the wilderness
and streams in the wasteland."
Isaiah 43:18-19 (NIV)

When we let go of past mistakes,
we can look forward to new beginnings.

Believe on the Lord Jesus Christ.

Surrender the mess to God, who is bigger than
our fears of repeating past mistakes
and our fears of facing the future.

Trust God, even when it's hard.

Because the true test of trust
doesn't happen in the easy.

Let's revoke the power we've given our regret
and experience the power of:

LOVE

the unconditional kind.

Maybe you didn't know that kind existed. It does.

Call upon the name of
the **LORD**

He loves you, and He delights in you.

His mercies are new every morning.
He makes all things new.

We are where we are,
at such a time as this,

for

a reason,

a purpose,

a plan…

Sure we could have taken that detour, made a different decision, taken that wise advice, but we didn't.

So here we are in this moment.

And when we surrender to God, love Him with all our heart, soul, and strength, and when we choose Jesus,

we are right where we are meant to be.

You are never alone.

PART IV

Taking the Next Step

God allows us
to experience trials and consequences,
not because He doesn't love us,
but because He does.

And we still have our memories,
but past mistakes don't define who we are.

Just like that woman at the well,

             our past can be used to bring hope.

Jesus loved her for who she was and didn't shun her for what she did. An encounter with her Lord and Savior changed everything. The same is true for me and for you.

Let's leave our shame and regret behind
and run into the city.
We all have a story to tell.

When we realize our past can be used
to change lives, it loses its bitterness
and its taste becomes sweet.

Let's change our perspective.
Our past has purpose.

God can transform
a mistake-ridden past
into a hope-filled future.

When we stop dwelling on past mistakes,
we free up room for a new way of thinking.

It's time for a renewing of our mind:

*"And do not be conformed to this world,
but be transformed by the renewing of your mind,
that you may prove what is that good and
acceptable and perfect will of God."*
Romans 12:2

So what shall we think on then?

What thoughts are pleasing to God?

"*Finally, brothers and sisters, whatever is true, whatever is noble, whatever is right, whatever is pure, whatever is lovely, whatever is admirable—if anything is excellent or praiseworthy— think about such things.*"

Philippians 4:8 (NIV)

God is the author of our story.

He breathes life into ashes and brings forth beauty, and His beauty is meant to be shared.

*It's time to forgive yourself
and allow God to use all of your story
for your good and His glory.*

So now beloved, the question is this:

Who will hear your story?

"'For I know the plans I have for you,' declares the LORD, 'plans to prosper you and not to harm you, plans to give you hope and a future…'"

Jeremiah 29:11 (NIV)

"Behold, I stand at the door and knock. If anyone hears My voice and opens the door, I will come in to him and dine with him, and he with Me."

Revelation 3:20

What's next?

Do you know Jesus?
Not just about Him, but really know Him as Lord and Savior?

For more information about meeting Jesus, check out the Meet Jesus tab at dorisswift.com/meet-Jesus

Pray for direction and head to a Bible-believing church. Discipleship is key in the journey of faith, and those who have walked this road for a good long time will be there to help and support you. If you've been away for awhile, they'll be ready to welcome you back.

Becoming a follower of Jesus will be the most important decision of your life. Blessings to you as you make this important step. Welcome to the family of God!

If this book has made an impact on your life in some way, I'd love to hear from you. Please connect with me at dorisswift.com, and click on the "Contact Me" tab.

Draw near to the Jesus, friend. He's waiting for you.

Acknowledgements

All glory and praises to God; He is faithful.

My sincere gratitude, love, and appreciation to:

My husband, Brian, who supports whatever I do and makes me feel loved every day. My family, who has encouraged, loved, and prayed for me. Love you forever.

Editor, Tara Cole, thank you for using your gifts to bless this project and for being an awesome encourager.

The *Goodbye, Regret* Book Launch Team. I am beyond blessed by your support, input, and all you have done to share about the book. Thank you for giving of your time.

My Walking Deeper community and Beta readers. Thank you for your comments, encouragement, and sharing about the book.

Jeff Goins, creator of Tribe Writers, who answered his calling by helping others find theirs, and to the Tribe Writer community who provided invaluable feedback. Blessed.

The staff at Edgewater Alliance Church, for their support, encouragement, and comments on the book.

The Thursday night group of God's girls I do life with. You mean the world to me. Thank you for your prayers and encouragement. We are family.

Made in the USA
Columbia, SC
05 December 2017